THE ASTROLABE, an instrument developed by the Greeks, is the symbol for JUNIOR WORLD EXPLORERS. At the time of Columbus, sailors used the astrolabe to chart a ship's course. The arm across the circle could be moved to line up with the sun or a star. Using the number indicated by the pointer, a sailor could tell his approximate location on the sea. Although the astrolabe was not completely accurate, it helped many early explorers in their efforts to conquer the unknown.

THE ASTROLABE, an instrument developed by the Greeks, is the symbol for JUNIOR WORLD EXPLORERS. At the time of Columbus, sailors used the astrolabe to chart a ship's course. The arm across the circle could be moved to line up with the sun or a star. Using the number indicated by the pointer, a sailor could tell his approximate location on the sea. Although the astrolabe was not completely accurate, it helped many early explorers in their efforts to conquer the unknown.

Junior World Explorers

Henry Morton Stanley

by Charles P. Graves
illustrated by Nathan Goldstein

Chelsea Juniors
A division of Chelsea House Publishers
New York ▪ Philadelphia

For Anne, Joe, and Neal Hodges

Cover Illustration: Katherine E. Craig

First Chelsea House edition 1991

1 3 5 7 9 8 6 4 2

ISBN   0-7910-1507-6

Contents

1. The Workhouse 5

2. The Runaway 11

3. America 19

4. John Finds a Father 24

5. Soldier and Reporter 34

6. "Find Livingstone!" 41

7. Africa 47

8. "Dr. Livingstone, I Presume" . . 54

9. Back to Africa 62

10. Down the Congo 71

11. "Breaker of Rocks" 81

12. Last Adventures 87

1

The Workhouse

The great door of the Workhouse banged shut as little John Rowlands was pulled inside. A tall, ugly man glared down at him.

"My name is James Francis," the man said. "I'm the schoolmaster here at the Workhouse. I'll try to hammer a little knowledge into your thick skull."

John was terrified as the schoolmaster led him upstairs. St. Asaph Union Workhouse was a home for orphans, unwanted children, and poor people. John had heard dreadful stories about it.

The Workhouse was in Wales, a part of Great Britain. John was born in Wales in 1841. Soon after John was born, his father died. His mother went to London to live and left John with her family. But nobody really wanted him. He was only six years old when he was put in the Workhouse.

The schoolmaster gave John a shabby gray uniform and made him put it on. Then he took John to a big room that had many beds. He pointed to one and said, "That's yours." John felt the bed. It was almost as hard as a rock.

At supper John sat at a long table with

many other boys. There was nothing to
eat except some watery oatmeal and a
little bread.

The boy across from John gulped his
oatmeal down. "We never get enough to
eat here," the boy said. Then he told John
that his name was Mose.

"Can't you ask for more?" John couldn't
believe that one bowl of oatmeal and a
little bread was the only food they would
have for supper.

"Mr. Francis would beat us if we did," Mose said.

That night the boys were locked into their room. When the lights were out, John cried himself to sleep.

The next morning the boys were awakened at six o'clock. They made the beds and swept the floors. Francis gave John a broom that was so heavy he could hardly lift it. But John was a hard worker. He wanted to succeed in everything he did. The harder the job was, the harder John worked.

After the chores were done, the children went to the schoolroom. Francis insisted that they pay strict attention. He had a quick temper and was always scolding the boys about something.

One day he was reading from the Bible. The chapter was about Joseph who told

the meaning of a king's dream. Suddenly,
Francis stopped reading and glared angrily
at John because he didn't think John was
listening.

"Who told the king what his dream
meant?" Francis demanded.

"Jophes, sir," John said.

"Who?" the schoolmaster shouted.

"Jophes, sir."

"Don't you mean Joseph?" Francis bel-
lowed with fury.

"Yes, sir," John said. "Jophes."

The schoolmaster was enraged because John couldn't pronounce "Joseph." He took his birch rod and rushed up to John.

John turned white with terror and stayed frozen in his seat. Francis grabbed the boy and beat him with the rod. John was hurt, but he didn't cry. He had learned that tears did no good in the Workhouse.

John got many other beatings. Once Francis beat him because he ate some blackberries. For the rest of his life, John thought of that beating each time he ate blackberries. He couldn't forget it even after his name was changed to Henry Morton Stanley, and he became a famous explorer.

2

The Runaway

The years went by slowly at the Workhouse. John kept hoping that someday someone would come and take him away. The other boys had visitors from time to time. But no one ever came to see John.

One day, when John was twelve years old, he heard that his mother had come to the Workhouse. John was filled with excitement.

At supper that night, John saw a tall woman with dark hair sitting at another table. The schoolmaster pointed to her.

"John," he asked, "do you know who that woman is?"

"No, sir," the boy answered.

"What! You don't know your own mother?"

John blushed and glanced hopefully at his mother. But she just stared at him coldly and then turned away. She didn't speak to him. John's heart almost broke.

His mother had come to the Workhouse to leave her daughter, John's half-sister. John never got to know his half-sister because the boys and girls were separated at the Workhouse.

By now John was getting used to disappointments and sorrow. He knew that if he was going to make a success of his life, he would have to do it all by himself. He started to work harder than ever at his lessons. Soon he was the best pupil.

He was also a born leader. Once the schoolmaster went on a trip and he put John in charge of the school.

When John was fifteen the Bishop of St. Asaph visited the school. He offered a prize to the boy who could draw the best. John had a special talent for drawing, and he won easily. The Bishop gave him a Bible. John kept this Bible with him all his life.

A short time after this a new table arrived at the school. One of the boys stood on it and scratched the top. When James Francis saw the scratches on the table, he went almost insane with rage.

Taking up a birch rod, he demanded to know who had scratched the table. No one would admit doing it.

"Very well, then," Francis said, "the entire class will get a beating."

The schoolmaster started beating the boys one by one. Soon it was John's turn. John was still small for his age, and Francis towered above him.

"You're next," Francis said. "I mean to stop this lying."

"I did not lie, sir," John said. "I know nothing about the scratches on the table."

"I'm going to beat you!" Francis roared.

"No!" John shouted. "Never again!"

Francis grabbed John by the collar and threw him on a bench. He struck John in the stomach and hit him hard on both cheeks.

John was weak with pain, but he was determined that Francis was not going to beat him again. He kicked the schoolmaster with all his might. Francis fell backward and hit his head on the stone floor. He was knocked out.

The boys dragged Francis to his study. They left him on the floor, shut the door, and ran to their room.

John's friend, Mose, turned to him and asked, "Do you suppose the schoolmaster is dead?"

John was worried. So he sent one of the boys to the study to find out if the schoolmaster was still alive. The boy came back and said that James Francis was bathing his face and that everything was all right.

Mose leaned toward John and whispered, "The master will have it in for you. Let's run away."

John agreed. He and Mose climbed over the garden wall and ran as fast as they could. Soon they were safely away from the Workhouse.

Mose had some family in a nearby town. They agreed to take Mose in. John knew he had a grandfather in the same town. "Maybe I can stay with him," John thought.

John went to see his grandfather. The old man was sitting in the kitchen, smoking a pipe.

"Who are you?" he asked.

"I am your grandson," the boy replied.

John's grandfather took the pipe from

his mouth and pointed toward the door. "You can go back the same way you came," he said. "I can do nothing for you and have nothing to give you."

John walked out of the house. Tears were in his eyes, but he held them back.

"No matter what happens," he said to himself, "I won't go back to the Workhouse."

3

America

John did not know what to do. How was he going to live? Finally a cousin who ran a school gave him a home. John became a pupil-teacher. He was not paid for his work. But at least he had a chance to get more education. He was quick to learn and was soon far ahead of the other pupils.

When John was seventeen he went to live in Liverpool, a big English seaport.

John was anxious to start earning money. He had been promised a job in an office. But, the promise of an office job was broken. John had to take a job at a butcher shop near the docks. He hated the work.

One day he delivered some meat to the captain of the *Windermere*, an American ship. John looked around and admired the captain's cabin.

"How would you like to sail on this ship?" the captain asked. "You could be my cabin boy."

"I know nothing of the sea, sir," John answered.

"You will soon learn," the captain said. "I will give you five dollars a month. In three days we sail for New Orleans."

John thought quickly. Five dollars a month was good pay in those days. Food on the ship would be free, and he could save all his pay.

"I will go with you, sir, if you think I can do the work."

John sailed for America. He had a bunk next to a boy named Harry. Harry had sailed on the *Windermere* before.

"The captain lied to you," Harry said. "You won't be his cabin boy. You'll have to work like a regular sailor."

John was angry about being cheated. But he couldn't do any work at first. He was very seasick.

One morning while he was lying in his bunk, moaning, he heard a voice yell at him from the deck.

"Step up here in a brace of shakes," the voice said, "or I'll come down and skin you alive."

Leaping out of his bunk, John rushed

up on deck. The second mate pointed to a broom. "Lay hold and sweep, you son of a sea cook," the mate shouted.

John grabbed the broom and started sweeping as fast as he could. He soon forgot about his seasickness. He was kept busy scrubbing decks and polishing brass.

Life on the ship was as hard as it had been at the Workhouse. The mates were cruel and swore at the men all the time. John was often kicked and beaten.

The *Windermere* sailed through several storms. Finally it reached the Gulf of Mexico. After a voyage of nearly two months, the ship docked at New Orleans.

John and Harry went ashore as soon as they could. John was so happy to be on land again that he did a dance.

4

John Finds a Father

In New Orleans John lived on the ship. He had to work all day long and could go ashore only at night.

The mates treated him even worse in New Orleans than they had at sea. They kicked him and cursed him from sunup to sundown.

"They're trying to make you leave without your pay," Harry said. "If they fire you, they'll have to pay you for two months' work. But if you quit, they won't have to pay you a penny."

Even so, John decided to leave. One night he took his Bible and went ashore. He was determined not to come back. He spent the rest of the night sleeping on some cotton bales.

John had no money. He had to find work immediately, or he would surely starve.

As soon as it was daylight he started looking for a job. He came to a building with a large sign that read "Speake and McCreary." A middle-aged man was sitting in front of the building reading a newspaper. John thought he might be Mr. Speake or Mr. McCreary.

"Do you want a boy, sir?" John asked.

"Eh," the man said, looking at John. "What did you say?"

"I want some work, sir. I asked if you wanted a boy."

"What work can you do?" the man asked in a kindly voice. "Can you read? What book is that in your pocket?"

"It is my Bible," John said, "a present from my bishop. Oh yes, sir, I can read!"

The man made John read part of his newspaper. Then he asked for a sample of John's handwriting. The man was pleased with John's neatness and skill. In those days most people had little education.

"I know Mr. Speake," the man said. "I'll recommend you for a job."

Mr. Speake said he would give John a week's trial at a salary of five dollars.

The man who recommended John was Henry Morton Stanley, a successful salesman. Mr. Stanley told John that he was going on a business trip, but would return shortly. "I hope to hear the best accounts of you," he said.

John worked hard. He moved groceries from inside the store to the sidewalk and marked them for shipping. He had a very good memory, and he soon knew where everything belonged. John swept the floors, too, both morning and night. At the end of the week Mr. Speake told John he liked his work. He hired him permanently at twenty-five dollars a month. This much money seemed like a fortune to John.

After he paid his rent at a boarding-house, he still had money left. He bought some clothes and then some books. One book was a big history of the United States. John did not know much about America, and he wanted to learn more.

When Mr. Stanley returned from his trip, he was pleased to find that John was doing so well. He invited the boy to have

Sunday breakfast with him and Mrs. Stanley.

After that first breakfast John saw more and more of the Stanleys. They had no children, and they enjoyed John's company. John liked the Stanleys too. Mrs. Stanley encouraged him to talk. She seemed interested in everything he said.

One day Mr. Stanley came to see John at the boardinghouse. He noticed the many books in John's room. The next day a big package arrived for John from Mr. Stanley. It contained a dozen new books. No one had ever been so kind to John before.

Once, while Mr. Stanley was on a trip, his wife became very sick. John went to help her. He even gave up his job so he could be with her day and night.

But there was nothing John could do to

help her get well. One night he was standing by her bed. She looked up at him and said, "Be a good boy. God bless you." Then she died.

When Mr. Stanley returned to New Orleans he learned how John had tried to help his wife. He was very grateful.

"Do you remember the first time I saw you?" Mr. Stanley asked John. "You came to me and asked, 'Do you want a boy, sir?' I have wanted a boy of my own all my life. But I thought you were too big to adopt. However, I've changed my mind." Mr. Stanley's voice shook with emotion. "Will you be my son?"

John could scarcely speak. "There's nothing I'd like better," he finally said.

Mr. Stanley put his arm around John. "In the future you are to bear my name," he said, "Henry Morton Stanley!"

Mr. Stanley had once been a minister. He stood up and dipped his hands in a basin of water. He made the sign of the cross on John's forehead and baptized him.

John had never been so happy. He had a father at last. Mr. Stanley was happy too, for he had a son. Now John Rowlands was Henry Morton Stanley.

Mr. Stanley and his adopted son began to travel up and down the Mississippi and Ohio Rivers on business trips. They went to Memphis, St. Louis, Cincinnati, and Louisville on big paddle-wheel riverboats.

When Henry was nineteen his father decided that he should go into business. "How would you like to be a merchant?" he asked.

"Fine," young Stanley said.

"It will be good training for you to

start working in a country store," his father said. "I can get you a job in Arkansas."

So Henry went to Arkansas, and Mr. Stanley went on a trip to Cuba. The father and son did not know that they would never see each other again.

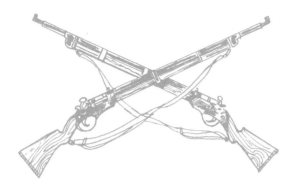

5

Soldier and Reporter

In Arkansas Henry was lonesome for his father. His father wrote to him at first. Then suddenly Mr. Stanley's letters stopped.

The Civil War had begun. Henry thought the war was keeping his father's letters from getting through. Several years later he learned that his father had died in Cuba about the time the war began.

Henry knew little about the causes of the war. He was not sure which side was right. But his friends were Southerners. So, he joined the Confederate Army.

His company was called the Dixie Greys. After training in Arkansas, the Dixie Greys went to war. At Shiloh, in Tennessee, the Confederates attacked a large Union Army.

Through the smoke of battle, Henry saw a long line of enemy soldiers. Fire was spitting from their rifles.

Henry and the other Dixie Greys advanced, firing as they went. Many men were killed or wounded. One bullet hit Stanley and knocked him down. Luckily the bullet struck his belt buckle, and he was not hurt. After dark the fighting stopped, and Stanley fell asleep on the ground, exhausted.

The next morning the battle started again. Stanley suddenly found himself surrounded by the enemy.

Six or seven Union soldiers pointed their rifles at him. "Down with that gun," one of them said, "or I'll drill a hole through you. Drop it! Quick!"

Stanley was taken to a prison camp near Chicago. The camp was dirty and crowded. The food was terrible, and there was almost no medical care.

Many prisoners died every day. Stanley was afraid he might die too.

One day a man who worked with Stanley at the prison camp said to him, "You can get out of here. All you have to do is join the Union Army."

"Oh, no!" Stanley said. "I could never do that. Most of my friends are Southerners."

But in a few weeks the horrors of the prison camp made Stanley change his mind. He felt that if he stayed any longer he would go crazy.

So Stanley joined the Union Army. After a few days he became sick. The Union Army discharged him.

Later, when he was well, he joined the United States Navy. His warship attacked a fort in North Carolina. When the battle was over Stanley wrote stories about it. He sent the stories to newspapers. The newspapers liked the way Stanley wrote, and they paid him well for his stories.

Stanley was almost twenty-four years old when the war ended. He decided to be a newspaper reporter. The work was interesting and exciting, and it gave him a chance to travel.

He went out West and wrote stories about the Indians. He was good at describing people and places, and he could make events sound exciting.

Stanley's dream was to get a job with a New York newspaper. Some of the best newspapers in the United States were in New York City. Henry Morton Stanley was already making a name for himself as a reporter. But he would not be satisfied until he was one of the best.

6

"Find Livingstone!"

When Stanley was twenty-seven he went to New York City. He asked James Gordon Bennett, Jr., the editor of *The New York Herald*, for a job.

Bennett had read some of Stanley's news stories. "I wish I could offer you something permanent," he said.

"A British Army is getting ready to invade Abyssinia," Stanley said. "Let me report the invasion for the *Herald*."

"If you will pay your own expenses," Bennett said, "I will give you a trial. If the stories you send back are good, I will hire you permanently."

"That's fine," Stanley said. He had saved enough money to pay his expenses, and he was sure Bennett would like his work. Stanley had become a cocky young man. "I've come a long way since I left the Workhouse," he often told himself.

On his way to Abyssinia (now called Ethiopia), Stanley stopped in Egypt. The telegraph office nearest to Abyssinia was there. Stanley made friends with the man who ran the office.

"When I return from Abyssinia," he said, "I'll pay you well if you'll send my stories ahead of all the others."

Stanley went with the British Army to Abyssinia. He saw the British win a big victory. He wanted to get the news back to the *Herald* as soon as possible.

He hurried back to Egypt by ship. When the ship reached Egypt, Stanley was not allowed to land. He hired a messenger to take his story of the British victory to the telegraph office.

The man who ran the office remembered Stanley's offer. He sent Stanley's story at once. Just after it was sent the cable under the Mediterranean Sea broke. No other stories went through for weeks.

The New York Herald had the news from Abyssinia long before any other paper in the world. It was a big scoop. It made Stanley a world-famous reporter.

James Gordon Bennett hired Stanley on a permanent basis. Stanley traveled about Europe reporting many important events.

Bennett's son followed Stanley's work closely. James Gordon Bennett, Jr., decided that Stanley was just the man to send to find Dr. David Livingstone. Livingstone was a famous British explorer and missionary who had disappeared in Africa.

In 1866 Livingstone had set out to find the source of the Nile River, one of the great mysteries of Africa. Since then, Livingstone had disappeared into the interior, and few letters had come from him. There were rumors that he had been killed by natives.

The Western world longed for news. *The New York Herald* wanted to supply that news.

"I think Livingstone is alive," James Gordon Bennett, Jr., told Stanley, "and that he can be found. I'm going to send *you* to find him."

Stanley was almost speechless.

"Do you really think I can find Livingstone?" he asked at last. "You want *me* to go to Central Africa?"

"Yes," young Bennett said.

"It will cost a great deal of money," Stanley remarked.

"I don't care what it costs!" Bennett cried. "FIND LIVINGSTONE!"

7

Africa

Stanley went to Zanzibar in January 1871. Zanzibar, an island off the east coast of Africa, was the expedition's starting point.

At Zanzibar, Stanley bought tons of supplies that he would need during his search for Livingstone. He bought guns and ammunition, tents, pots and pans, rope, and medicine.

He learned that money was worthless in the middle of Africa. The native chiefs made travelers pay in goods to pass through their lands. So Stanley bought cloth, wire, and beads to use as money.

Stanley hired many Africans to go on the trip. Some were soldiers. Others were porters who would carry the supplies.

When everything was ready, the men sailed from Zanzibar to the African mainland. Then the expedition started toward

Ujiji, more than 700 miles away. Livingstone's last letter had come from there.

Most of the soldiers and porters had to walk. But Stanley rode on a fine bay horse. A large American flag flew above his caravan.

The expedition moved slowly. Sometimes Stanley and his men had to chop their way through thick tropical jungles. It was unbearably hot. Poisonous insects bit them. Then Stanley's horse died.

Stanley became very sick with tropical fever. Sometimes he had to stay in his tent for several days. His temperature was often 105 degrees. When he was sick, he read his Bible for comfort.

No matter how sick Stanley was, he had to be alert. He could not trust anyone else to lead the expedition. Most of the men were brave and honest. But some deserted and others disobeyed. Slowly, Stanley learned to handle them.

When the expedition reached Tabora, an Arab town 200 miles from the coast, Stanley stopped to rest.

One of the Arabs gave Stanley a little African boy as a servant. His name was Ndugu M'hali, but Stanley thought the boy should have a better name.

"How about 'Kalulu'?" someone suggested. "That's African for little antelope."

"That's perfect," Stanley said. He baptized the little boy with the words, "Let his name henceforth be Kalulu, and let no man take it from him."

Stanley liked children, and Kalulu was a joy to him. He was a bright boy, and he learned fast. Kalulu liked to bring Stanley his food at mealtimes.

While at Tabora, Stanley learned that the shortest way to Ujiji was blocked by a chief named Mirambo. Mirambo said he would destroy any caravan that tried to pass through his land.

"We'll go around Mirambo," Stanley said finally. This meant a long, hard detour to the south. Some of the men on the expedition were discouraged. But Stanley was not. "My job is to find Livingstone," he said, "and I will do it."

One day Stanley met some natives who had come from Ujiji. They told Stanley that a gray-bearded white man was staying there.

"That must be Livingstone!" Stanley said. "We must hurry and get there before he leaves."

Stanley longed for a horse. With a horse he could get to Ujiji much faster.

Stanley didn't have much patience left. So he promised his men that he would give them extra pay if they would march to Ujiji without a day's rest. The men agreed.

The expedition raced toward Ujiji. One night a native chief told Stanley that Ujiji was only a short march away.

"Tomorrow I'll find Livingstone!" Stanley said to himself before falling asleep.

8

"Dr. Livingstone, I Presume"

Stanley woke before dawn the next morning. He was too excited to sleep any longer.

He had his men change into clean clothes. Stanley wanted everyone to look his best for the march into Ujiji.

The expedition climbed a steep hill, and Stanley gazed in wonder at the scene below. There, gleaming like silver in the sunshine, was Lake Tanganyika. Ujiji was on the shore of the lake.

As the caravan neared Ujiji, the Africans started shouting and singing.

"Load your guns!" Stanley said. It was the custom in Africa to announce a caravan's arrival by firing guns in the air.

"One, two, three—fire!" Stanley ordered. Nearly fifty guns fired a salute. Kalulu acted as Stanley's gunbearer.

"March!" Stanley cried.

As the caravan moved forward, the people in Ujiji rushed out to greet the strangers.

"Bindera Merikani—the American flag!" the people cried. *"Yambo!" Yambo* means "how are you?"

An African dressed in a long white shirt came up to Stanley. "Good morning, sir," he said in perfect English.

"Who are you?" Stanley asked with a smile.

"I am Susi," the man replied, "the servant of Dr. Livingstone."

"Run and tell the doctor I am coming," Stanley said.

As Susi dashed off, Stanley's heart started pounding with joy and excitement. He ordered the caravan to move on. Just ahead, Stanley saw a group of Arabs surrounding a white man with a gray beard.

Stanley wanted to run to the old man. He was so happy that he had found the doctor at last. But he was afraid Livingstone might not like that. So Stanley walked toward him slowly and with dignity.

He took off his hat and said, "Doctor Livingstone, I presume."

"Yes," Livingstone said.

The two men shook hands. "I thank God, Doctor, that I have been permitted to see you."

"I feel thankful," Livingstone said, "that I am here to welcome you."

Livingstone invited Stanley to come to the hut where he lived. He was eager for news of the outside world. Livingstone was fifty-eight years old, but he looked much older. Life in Africa had been hard on his health.

He told Stanley that he had been sick and had run out of supplies. He had sent letters home, but they had probably been lost on the way. Letters from Ujiji had to be carried by hand for hundreds of miles to the coast.

Stanley spent several months with Livingstone. They explored the northern end of Lake Tanganyika together and became good friends. Livingstone was kind and gentle, and he reminded Stanley of his father, Mr. Stanley.

"Won't you come back to Europe with me?" Stanley asked one day.

"There are still several parts of Africa that I want to explore," Livingstone said.

"Haven't you done enough?" Stanley argued.

"No," Livingstone said. "There is a river far to the west called the Lualaba. I think it is the Nile River."

"Couldn't it be the beginning of the Congo River?" Stanley asked.

"It could be," Livingstone said. "But an explorer must follow it to the sea to find out. I want to be that explorer."

Stanley promised to send Livingstone supplies to help him continue his explorations. Then he said good-bye and led his caravan back to Zanzibar.

After he had paid his men, he sailed for Europe. Kalulu went with him.

Stanley felt sure that he would return to Africa some day. "Africa," he said, "is in my blood."

9

Back to Africa

On his way back to Europe, Stanley received a message from James Gordon Bennett, Jr. "You are now as famous as Livingstone," Bennett wrote, "having discovered the discoverer."

But to Stanley's bitter disappointment, when he reached England, the newspapers made fun of him. They did not believe that he had found Livingstone. How could a newspaper reporter, and an American at that, lead an expedition into the heart of Africa? Many Englishmen thought Stanley was lying.

Livingstone had given Stanley his diary and some letters for his family. The Livingstones said they believed Stanley. Gradually other people came to believe him too.

Queen Victoria sent him a gold snuffbox covered with diamonds. This was her way of thanking Stanley for finding Britain's famous explorer. The Royal Geographical Society awarded him the Victoria Medal, their highest honor.

Stanley put Kalulu in an English boarding school and went back to his work as a reporter. One day he heard that Livingstone had died in Africa.

"Dear Livingstone," Stanley wrote in his notebook, "another sacrifice to Africa. His mission must not be allowed to cease; others must go forward and fill the gap. . . ."

Stanley himself wished to be the one to fill the gap. He longed to go back to Africa and prove that he was a real explorer as well as a good reporter.

He bought more than 130 books about Africa and studied them carefully. Then he went to see the editor of a London newspaper, *The Daily Telegraph.*

"Livingstone did not live to complete his work in Africa," Stanley said.

"What needs to be done?" the editor asked.

"There are still three great mysteries on the map of Africa," Stanley explained. "First, Lake Victoria. Is it one lake or is it several lakes? Second, does Lake Tanganyika have an outlet? And third, is the Lualaba River the same as the Nile? Or is it really the Congo? We must know the answers to these questions before we can fill in the blank spaces on the map of Africa."

"Could you solve these mysteries?" the editor asked.

"If I live long enough," Stanley replied.

James Gordon Bennett, Jr., agreed to help the London newspaper pay for an expedition to Africa.

Stanley set to work at once making plans. He hired three young Englishmen to go with him. They were Frederick Barker, and Edward and Francis Pocock. Stanley was impressed by Barker's eagerness and determination. He hired the Pococks because they were good at handling small boats. He would need their skills on the lakes and rivers.

Stanley had one boat built in five different sections. The pieces could be carried through the African jungles, then

put together when the expedition reached water. Stanley named the boat the *Lady Alice*.

In the summer of 1874 Stanley, the three Englishmen, and Kalulu sailed for Zanzibar. Kalulu was now about thirteen years old. He was strong for his age, and Stanley thought he would be a big help on the expedition.

At Zanzibar, Stanley bought tons of supplies and hired 356 Africans and Arabs to go with him. In the middle of November the expedition started for Lake Victoria.

It was a hard trip. Some of the men died of the heat. Others died of typhus, and Edward Pocock was one of them. This was a great loss to Stanley.

When the expedition reached Lake Victoria, Stanley had the *Lady Alice* put together. Stanley and a few natives set out to explore the lake.

They sailed all around it, and Stanley made careful maps. He proved it was one big lake and not several small ones as some people thought. Lake Victoria is the second largest fresh-water lake in the world.

When Stanley rejoined the expedition, he heard some more bad news. Frederick Barker had died suddenly. Now Stanley and Francis Pocock were the only white men left with the expedition.

With a sad heart, Stanley led his men to Lake Tanganyika. He sailed around it and proved that it had no outlet.

Now the *Lady Alice* was taken apart again. It had to be carried more than 200 miles to the Lualaba River.

Stanley found an Arab who lived near

the river. "Tell us what you know of this river," Stanley said.

"It flows north," the Arab said.

"And then?" asked Stanley.

"It flows north and north and north. I think it reaches the Salt Sea."

"But what Salt Sea?" Stanley asked himself. "If the river flows into the Mediterranean, it is the Nile. If it flows into the Atlantic, it must be the Congo."

The Arab told Stanley that the river flowed through country inhabited by cannibals. There were leopards, boa constrictors, and crocodiles along its banks.

Stanley knew that a dangerous journey lay ahead. He and many of his men might be killed. But nothing could stop him now. He was determined to follow the river to its mouth and finish the work started by Livingstone.

10

Down the Congo

Stanley and his men started along the eastern bank of the Lualaba River. They had to cut paths through the thick forest. It was slow work.

"It will take us forever to follow the river by land," Stanley said. "We must travel on the river itself."

Stanley had the *Lady Alice* put together again. He captured some canoes from natives and bought others.

Cannibals lived in villages on the banks of the river. Stanley had two men who could speak their language. When the boats passed a cannibal village, the men would shout, *sennenneh*, which means peace.

One day, as they neared a village, the natives started beating drums and shouting a war cry. Cannibals in giant canoes

paddled swiftly toward the *Lady Alice* and Stanley's other boats.

One of the cannibals hurled a spear at Stanley. It flew over his head and landed in the water. Stanley and his men started shooting. The cannibals had never seen nor heard guns before. They fled in terror.

Stanley had to fight many more battles.

Some of his men were killed and many were wounded. But Stanley did not give up. For many miles the river flowed north. Then it curved to the west. Stanley knew now that it could not be the Nile. "It must be the Congo," he decided.

Weeks and months passed by as the expedition went slowly down the river. The water started flowing faster and faster. There were many dangerous rapids and waterfalls. Sometimes the *Lady Alice* and the canoes had to be carried around the falls. Roads had to be hacked through the jungles and forests. Sometimes it took all day to go a few hundred yards.

There were some terrible accidents. The expedition's best canoe was swept over a waterfall and wrecked. Fortunately, no one was in it.

One day Stanley heard roaring water ahead. He knew it was another dangerous waterfall. He sent some men ahead to explore the land. They came back and said there was a fine camping ground a short distance away.

Stanley decided to try to reach it. The falls were in the middle of the river below the camping ground. The water was calm close to the banks. Stanley thought that by staying close to the bank the canoes could reach the camp ground safely.

There were now only seventeen canoes left. Not everyone could go in the canoes. Some people would have to walk. The strongest paddlers were needed so that the canoes would not be swept into the middle of the river and over the falls.

As Stanley climbed into the *Lady Alice*,

he noticed that Kalulu was in a canoe called the *Crocodile.*

"Kalulu!" Stanley shouted. "What are you doing in the canoe?"

Kalulu smiled proudly. "I can paddle, sir," he said. "See!" The boy grabbed a paddle and pulled it smoothly through the water.

"All right," Stanley said. "You may go in the canoe." Stanley warned all the paddlers to keep the canoes close to the bank. "By no means," he said, "go into the current."

The *Lady Alice* hugged the bank and reached the camping ground safely. Three canoes arrived soon afterward. Stanley thought all was well.

Suddenly, to his horror, he saw a canoe in the middle of the river. It was the *Crocodile,* bearing his precious Kalulu.

With the speed of an arrow, the *Crocodile* flew toward the falls. Wild water boiled and foamed around it.

Kalulu and the men in the canoe paddled with all their might, but the current was too swift. As the canoe neared the falls it whirled around several times. Then it leaped into the air and plunged over the falls. Kalulu and the other paddlers were crushed to death on the rocks below.

Stanley was heartbroken. As a memorial to his lost son, he named the place Kalulu Falls.

A few weeks later Francis Pocock's canoe went over another waterfall, and he was killed. Now Stanley was the only white man left with the expedition. He worked harder than ever to lead his men to the mouth of the Congo.

As they neared the sea the natives they met were more friendly. But they refused to sell Stanley any food. Stanley and his men were slowly starving.

One day a native told Stanley that he was only a six-days' journey by water from Boma, a town near the mouth of the river. But there were waterfalls ahead. Stanley and his men were too weak from hunger to carry their boats around the falls.

So the expedition left the river and went on by land. "We'll get to Boma," Stanley said, "if we don't starve first."

Stanley wrote a note and sent it to Boma by three of his strongest men. The note asked anyone who could read English to send help at once. "Starving people cannot wait," the note said.

A few days later help came. The people

in Boma sent rice, fish, and sweet potatoes. Stanley's expedition was saved.

When Stanley and his men regained their strength, they marched on to Boma. They arrived there on August 9, 1877. This was the 999th day since they had left Zanzibar.

Now Stanley's mission was over. He had solved the last great mystery of Africa. The Lualaba was the Congo, and it flowed into the Atlantic Ocean.

Stanley's heart was filled with joy at his success, but his eyes were filled with tears. He could not forget the many friends he had lost while following the river.

11

"Breaker of Rocks"

Stanley was sorry when he had to leave his brave African friends. As he wrote later, "Aided by their willing hands and by their loyal hearts, the expedition had been successful. . ."

When Stanley returned to Europe, he was the world's most famous living explorer. Many people came to hear his lectures about the Congo. He wrote books about the expedition. He included drawings he had made of Africa.

"I believe the natives could be civilized if the Congo were opened up for trade," he said. He tried to get the English to build trading posts along the river. They were not interested.

But the King of the Belgians, Leopold II, was interested. He sent Stanley back to the Congo.

In 1879 Stanley started up the Congo River from the Atlantic coast. He and his helpers traveled in four little steamers.

When they reached the falls Stanley said, "We must build roads around them. That's the only way we can carry our supplies to the upper part of the Congo."

The roads had to be built with crushed rock. Stanley gave his native helpers some sledgehammers. The natives didn't know how to use them.

"Here, let me show you," Stanley said, picking up a sledgehammer. He swung the heavy tool over his head and brought it down on a big rock. Crash! The rock broke into many small pieces. "See how easy it is," Stanley said proudly.

The natives were astonished at Stanley's strength. "We're going to call you *Bula Matari*," one of the natives said.

"What does *Bula Matari* mean?" Stanley asked.

"Breaker of rocks," the native said. Stanley was pleased with his new name.

Bula Matari worked along the Congo for almost six years. He started many trading stations. The natives brought ivory, coffee, rubber, and other African products to the stations. They traded them for cloth, beads, guns, and other European goods. Slowly the natives learned the ways of the outside world.

Someday, Stanley hoped, the outside world would allow the people of the Congo to govern themselves. He was shocked when he learned that Leopold II was selling the Africans' land to European companies. Some of the Europeans treated the Africans like slaves. Stanley thought that the Africans should be free.

He did not live to see his dream come true. But today the natives along the Congo are free men. They live in a nation called the Republic of the Congo. One of its most important cities was then named Stanleyville. There is a statue of Stanley by the Congo River.

12

Last Adventures

Africa was still in Stanley's blood. He loved the wild and beautiful land. In 1887 he learned that another European was trapped in Africa. Stanley offered to help him. The man was a German who had changed his name to Emin Pasha.

Emin Pasha had been trying to help Egypt in a war with some Sudan natives. He had a small army, but it was not strong enough to beat the Sudanese. Emin Pasha had retreated to Central Africa. He could not find his way through the jungles to the sea.

So Stanley went to rescue him. Stanley led an expedition up the Congo River. It was the largest expedition he had ever commanded.

Many of the Africans on the expedition had been with Stanley before. He now spoke their language. This made him popular with the Africans.

The expedition went up the Congo as far as it could. Then Stanley left the river with a small group of picked men. He hoped they could reach Emin Pasha quickly.

Stanley led his men into a thick forest. He called it a "region of horrors." There were ticks, ants, and mosquitoes. There were giant snakes and man-eating animals.

Many men, including Stanley, became sick with malaria. Stanley was suffering, but he drove his men on.

One night Stanley camped near a native village.

In the middle of the night he was awakened by wild cries. There seemed to be two voices.

In an African language the first voice screamed, "Where are you going?"

Like an echo the second voice repeated, "Where are you going?"

"All men will be against you," the first voice said.

"Against you . . ." repeated the echo.

"And you will surely be slain."

"Surely slain . . ."

"Ah-ah-ah-ah-ah . . . Ooh-ooh-ooh . . ."

Some of Stanley's men laughed. They knew the natives were trying to scare them. However, these natives were really dangerous. They often shot poisoned arrows at the expedition. Stanley's men shot back with their guns.

It was taking much longer than Stanley had expected to go through the forest. In some places he sank up to his knees in mud. It took an hour to go a few hundred yards.

Day after day and week after week, the expedition plodded on. In the daytime the African heat was fierce. At night it often rained, and the men shivered around their campfires.

In spite of the many hardships Stanley found time to keep notebooks. He wrote

about the animals and the native tribes he saw.

He was particularly interested in the Pygmies. He noted that full-grown Pygmies were between three and four-and-a-half feet tall.

Stanley not only wrote about the natives, but he drew many pictures of them. He also made maps so that future explorers to the heart of Africa would have an easier time.

It was on the shores of Lake Albert that Stanley finally found Emin Pasha.

"I owe you a thousand thanks, Mr. Stanley," Emin Pasha said.

Stanley led Emin Pasha and his army safely to the coast. Stanley had now crossed Africa from west to east. He had explored much new land. During the journey he discovered the Mountains of

the Moon and Lake Edward. The blank spaces on the map of Africa were now all filled in.

But at what a cost! More than 500 of Stanley's men had died or had been lost on the trip. Stanley's health was wrecked. He was never really strong again.

When Stanley returned to England he settled down at last. He married an artist named Dorothy Tennant.

He took Dorothy to America. He tried to show her the house in New Orleans where he had lived, but he couldn't find it.

After the Stanleys returned to England, they adopted a baby boy. They named him Denzil. Stanley could hardly wait until the baby grew old enough to play games and read books.

When Denzil was nine years old, Stanley became desperately ill. He cheered up

when Denzil came to the hospital to see him.

"Father, are you happy?" Denzil asked.

"Always when I see you," Stanley said.

But nothing could help Stanley now. He died a few days later.

A huge block of stone was placed over his grave. The inscription on it says:

HENRY MORTON
STANLEY
Bula Matari
1841–1904
AFRICA

Stanley did not need the stone over his grave to be remembered. The map of Africa is his monument.